I'm Knot Ready!

Get Ready To Learn New Rules To An Old Game.

By
Mama Jr.

Copyright © 2021 Mama Jr.

All Rights reserved. This book or any portion thereof may not be reproduced or used in any manner whatsoever without the express written permission of the publisher except for the use of brief quotations in a book review.

ISBN (978-1-7366988-0-8)

Editing by: Bethany Davis

Book design by: Kozakura

Printed and bound in the United States of America.
First Printing, April 2021.

Published by Helpmate Publishing, LLC
Raleigh, North Carolina, USA

Visit www.mamajr.com

Father God: Thank you. Thank you for every lesson and every triumph. I am so humbled to have been given the ability, opportunity, vision and means to complete this project. My life's goal is to make you proud of me.

Mickey Daddy: I love you and miss you immensely. Rest in Peace.

Darlene: I could write an entire book on the things you have taught me about being a woman. I am proud that I get to be your daughter and represent you. I embrace my feisty, warm, loving, humorous, crafty, B-S detecting self because it is a DIRECT extension of you. I love and appreciate you.

Anna Fay, Deborah, Wanda, Carrie, Cecilia and Kelly: Thank you so much for showing me how it's done. The gifts you've given are priceless and have shown me how to be a lady. Spiritual, Resilient, Proud, Loving, Fierce and Classy. I don't know if you realized that I've been taking notes, but I have. Thank you.

Odie and Qwen: I was your Mama Jr. first (whether you wanted me to be or not)! Thank you SO much for trusting your big-little sister. It means so much to me.

I am so very proud of the men that you've grown to be and the awesome things to come.

Michael: I thank you for sparking the flame that made Mama Jr. official. You saw something in me and thought the world would like to see it as well. Your support, love, peace and encouragement make me better. You are an amazing man and I love that I get to love you.

XOXO

-Mama Jr.

Two roads diverged in a wood, and I-
I took the one less traveled by,
And that has made all the difference.

Excerpt from "The Road Not Taken" by Robert Frost.

Table of Contents

Introduction
p.9

Chapter 1 - Successfully Single
p.18

Chapter 2 - Know Why You Even Want to Be Married
p.44

Chapter 3 - Learn How To Date
p.62

Chapter 4 - Is Your Steady Ready
p.84

Chapter 5 - Patience My Friend…Patience
p.108

Chapter 6 - Family & Friends
p.124

Chapter 7- Are You Marriage Material
p.143

Conclusion
p.158

Acknowledgements

To my AR's: Ta'Quasha Felix, Dequandra Gilbert, Erica Johnson, Michael Jones, Janaya McFarlin, Stephanie Patterson and LaTisha Walter, THANK YOU!!! Your input has been invaluable and I greatly appreciate your time, attention, confidentiality and constructive criticism for this project.

Special Thanks

Mom, Mike, NaNa, Rochelle and Heather, thank you so much for your support and feedback along the way.

To the reader,

Please leave a book review and visit my Mama Jr. YouTube channel for more advice and commentary. Please tell someone about this book or gift it to someone. Thank you so much for your support.

Introduction

How bad do you want it? What have you considered doing in order to meet "the one"?

For years we have watched reality shows about single men and women tossing around candidates left and right in an effort to find their forever love. Tell me you haven't thought about putting in an application for the show, *Married at First Sight*? (I didn't say you did, but you've thought about it, haven't you? Uh huh, I knew it.)

Don't feel bad, I can absolutely relate. A few years ago when this show came out, you thought about how bold those folks were and how there was no way you would ever do something like that! (At least not on national TV, right?) Then you begin thinking it wouldn't hurt if you just went ahead and applied for the show. I mean … what're the odds of you getting matched with someone, anyway? After that, you start to watch more episodes, peek at the website, see the application requirements, find out where the next taping will be and before you know it, BOOM! Maybe you and your friends are standing in line when the show comes to your town.

I remember being similarly skeptical about online dating, and guess where I ended up meeting my man?

Nowadays, online dating is more popular than meeting somebody at the grocery store. Every day thousands of people are on Plenty of Fish, Zoosk, Match and Tinder looking for everything from hookups to lifelong partners. I'm so glad I paid for my three months on eHarmony, because that's where I met my boo.

Look, I know you're tired of the foolishness and just want to be married already. I know you have been thinking about what it would be like to actually meet someone who gets you and wants nothing more than to spend the rest of their life with you. You've been preparing for your happily ever after since Cinderella got hers. Well, throw away the fairy tale books, honey! It's about to get real. We need to talk about what you have been doing wrong and why you haven't found "the one" (or why "the one" hasn't found you). Yes, I said what *you* have been doing wrong—because you're the one choosing the duds.

I know it makes you feel better to say "Ain't no good men out here. They're either dead or in jail." Sure, some of this may be true, but I refuse to believe God didn't make one suitable partner for you out of the billions of people on this earth.

It's about time you realized that there are some things you just can't control when it comes to finding your spouse. However, there are some things you *can* control when it comes to *you*. I'm not talking about putting on a facade; I am talking about just the opposite. I'm talking about being your true self unapologetically and feeling great about the person that you attract as you are.

Part of the problem is that folks are attracted to the *public you*, and they are not attracted to the *private you*. When this happens, it's easy to become offended and hurt when things are no longer working out. You don't understand what happened, because things were going so well at the beginning. Well, in the beginning they didn't know half of your body parts were ordered from Amazon, or that your cooking experience was limited to what your microwave could nuke! Then you're sitting there with an attitude, telling people, "He should've known!" Well, he didn't, and that's why he peaced out! You need to find happiness within you so you can have the conversation early on that let's your potential partners know some of your features have been enhanced or that cooking is not one of your strong suits. Of course, these are just two examples.

Also, I need you to understand being single is not a death sentence. Some of you are actually waiting to get married so your lives can begin. You keep talking about when you get married; you're going to do this and that. If you are putting off the things you enjoy because you aren't in a relationship, then you're playing yourself! What if your spouse doesn't want to do the things you've been putting off? Baby, you betta start living!

You ought to know that you can not script life. If you could, wouldn't you be married to the fine celebrity that you have a crush on?! You can't anticipate when you are going to meet the person that you will marry. You cannot anticipate their background, how many children they may have or what they do for a living. When you do get married, it will be filled with unexpected highs and lows.

I'm Knot Ready

If you think back to your early childhood, there have been countless movies, television programs and fictional stories that have allowed us to paint this picture of grandeur as it pertains to marriage and how it will save us all. Think about it: most romantic comedies give you a two-hour tale of some single person screwing up their life or being noticeably unfulfilled. Towards the middle of the movie, they realize they have found "the one". They screw up a little bit more, which puts them in danger of losing this amazing catch, and finally all of their woes end when "the catch" realizes they can't live without the main character. The story eventually comes to an end as we witness a grandiose wedding between the two. As the viewer, we walk away in a trance with the sound of harps playing as we are left to think, *why can't that happen to me?*

As we become adults and begin exploring our own relationships, we realize that getting married is an uphill battle. Either we find someone who wants us and we don't want them, or we want someone who doesn't want us. We spend years with a person who has no intention of marrying us and then we resent the time spent even though they never made any promises to begin with. As time progresses, we become anxious, thinking about the possibility of never finding the magical key that is supposed to unlock our happiness, and start trying to force any and everyone to be *the* one.

I remember thinking the hardest part would be finding someone who loved me enough to want to be married to me. Then, I got married. I realized my fantasies about marriage allowed me to be ill-prepared when choosing a partner as well as ill-informed about what to expect within the relationship. Back when I was a single woman, marriage to me was all about the wedding—and I know I'm not alone! No matter how much I could articulate the difference, anytime I thought about being married, my mind went straight to my wedding day, or preparing for it. My whole idea of marriage was set on that one day.

I wanted to write this book in hopes of getting you out of the mindset that marriage will somehow make your life perfect or the belief that marriage is just about the wedding, because it's not. I want you to continue to strive for marriage, but with a realistic view.

This book will confront your misconceptions about marriage and help you to identify why your ring finger is still bare. You will be challenged to work on your shortcomings and take charge of your own happiness instead of expecting some mystery person to be responsible for it. I want you to understand that your marriage will be what you make of it, and no matter how tired you are of hearing it, communication truly *is* the key.

This book should be used as a guide, not a relationship bible. It will help you to realize there are some things you can do differently regarding the way you think and how you present yourself in relationships. I want you to continue to be open to marriage, but be very clear about the fact that your wedding ring will not fix your problems or magically create happiness. Married or not, those things will always be left up to you.

So, are you ready for an overdose of reality? Not to worry, this overdose is sure to leave you sober and truly prepared to be married.

Chapter 1

Successfully Single

I want to begin this book that will discuss your interest in being married by addressing your current status: SINGLE! Repeat after me, "I am single and that is okay! I am single and that is okay!" Just teasing… had to start you off with a little humor, because I wrote this book to calm you down and remind you there is nothing wrong with you or where you may be in life. It is very important to address being single because, as we've heard so many times before, it's hard to know where you're going if you don't know where you've been— or in your case, where you currently are!

So many of us are single, but when it is not by choice, we refuse to focus on it and we dare not attempt to enjoy it. We act like it is a disgrace to be single and some of us are actually ashamed of it. Because of this notion that something is wrong with being single, many of us jump from one meaningless relationship to another just to say you have a significant other, no matter how unfulfilled or downright unhappy we may be with this person. Now repeat after me: "Being single is nothing to be ashamed of!" You didn't say it did you? I knew it. That's cool though, just stay with me. Being single has nothing to do with how attractive or how worthy you are. It simply means you are not in a committed relationship, and you must embrace the fact that that's absolutely fine! It is... I promise!

In this chapter, I want you to understand how to be successfully single. I know you think that since you are already single, you've mastered how to do it, but I'm going to challenge your thinking. When you are done with this chapter, I want you to know how to be a happy, fulfilled individual whose life has meaning, joy and purpose— and yes, is also single. I want to challenge you to stop identifying yourself as *single* and go back to identifying yourself as the person whose name is on your birth certificate. Understanding how to be successfully single requires self-reflection. This will allow you to understand who you are and where you are in life.

If you're looking for a partner, you need to know what you bring to the table. Often we are able to give every detail of what we want as it pertains to our perfect mate. We know how tall or how thin or thick we want them to be. We know the education we'd like them to have, the way they should wear their hair, the type of job we'd like them to have, and what car we'd like them to drive. On the other hand though, when it comes to selling ourselves to someone else, most of us can only say, "I'm a female of a certain age, I'm from this part of the country and I do such and such for a living".

REALLY?! This is the dynamic information that your prince charming is supposed to be excited about?

During your time as a single person you should be figuring out who you are and what you do and don't like. Yes, I said it! This is the part where you recognize and accept who you really are, so you don't get into a relationship and start giving your new partner a hard time because they couldn't guess what would make you happy. Because of the work you are about to do on yourself, you will be able to tell your new boo what your interests are and stop playing childish games. See, your future relationship is getting better already! We just avoided the argument that would've surely ruined date night! You're welcome.

So, let's talk about why you are single. Most of us have been in a relationship or two that we can reference and come up with reasons as to why the relationship did not work out, but there are some people who are reading this book who have never been in a relationship for one reason or another, and that is fine too. I'm still talking to you all; don't think you're exempt from this portion of the book.

For those of you who have always been single, I want you to think about why you've never been in a relationship. What stopped you from making a commitment? If you're under eighteen years old, you don't need to answer this question. Your focus should have been and should *still* be on your education. Trust me, relationships are stressful honey, and the longer you wait to start that chapter of your life, the better off you'll be! And that first love is a doozy baby, let me tell you! (Yes, I said doozy! I will surely show my age throughout this book, it is what it is). In *my* opinion, your first love always seems to be with the wrong person, at the wrong time, and for the wrong reason. Then you look back years later and think, *I was such a mess for clinging to that joker. I'm so glad I've grown!*

For those of us who have been in relationships before, unless your first love was a few months ago, I truly hope you can say that you've grown since that experience. If not, you've got some work to do. As for the rest of you who have been around the block a time or two, what happened? Think about how many relationships you've been in. Count them. *All of them.* Yep, even that one! If you have been in more than five relationships, write them down. Really think about why each relationship ended and, because you are doing this without an audience, you can actually go ahead and admit if it was your fault! Don't count the people you only dated; I am speaking of the individuals that you were in a mutually-agreed-upon monogamous relationship with. Sorry boo, but the crush you used to "go with" in elementary school for two weeks does not count!

Now, as you are thinking back, think about why the relationship ended. Then pay attention to whether or not there were any similarities in why different relationships ended. People often think back and recognize they are always getting lied to, cheated on, financially used, emotionally and/or physically abused or just downright disrespected. You must pay attention to whether or not there have been patterns in those relationships so you can decide that the last time those things happened was the last time they're going to happen!

If there were relationships you can admit ended because you were primarily at fault, look for the commonalities there as well. Why do you continue to behave this way in relationships? Why do you continue to start new relationships, treat the person badly and then expect them to stay? Or do you not actually expect them to? Are you intentionally sabotaging your relationships? Why get into relationships if you know this is what will happen? One reason some of us keep dating individuals that have the same negative characteristics is because of a reason you may not be aware of: *they are just like our parents*. I know this is the part where you think, *this lady has lost her mind*, but hear me out. There are several pieces of information right at your fingertips that will support the idea that we tend to subconsciously choose partners with the same characteristics as our parents. Ladies, you may have witnessed your father being an abusive man in one way or another and, sure enough, all you come across are abusive men. This is not to say you *want* to be in these types of relationships, but they represent your foundation, what is familiar, and unless you make the conscious effort to avoid those types of relationships, you can very easily find yourself connecting with people like this again and again.

On the other hand though, there are people who are intentionally seeking partners with their parents' characteristics because they adore their parents and saw healthy, successful relationships while growing up. I know men who feel like they would be lucky to find a woman who works hard and takes care of her family like their moms did for them. Likewise, there are women who feel like they deserve a man that will provide and cherish them in the same way they saw their fathers do with their moms. If you have identified that many of your past partners had some similar characteristics, then ladies think about whether or not your father possessed those traits. Once you think about it, you may be surprised that some of your exes actually were a dead ringer for your dad. Don't feel bad, though! You don't know what you don't know.

I'm one of those people who married a man who had many characteristics like my father. Obviously, I didn't realize that at the time, but when I sat and thought about it later on, they both were extremely popular men who were the life of the party (to say the least). After I realized that I had not only dated, but married a man like my father (I was divorced by this time), I was determined to look for a different type of man. To me, there is nothing wrong with a well-liked, lively person. Those were actually traits that I liked about both my father and my ex-husband. As I made my comparison list however, I realized there were some traits that my father and my ex-husband shared that I absolutely did not find attractive. Because I didn't pay attention or accept that the glimpses of those traits would only grow in time, I ended up divorcing that well-liked, lively man.

Of course, this is not the only reason we choose incompatible partners. It's just one of many potential reasons, but I thought I'd mention it because of how often it happens.

Now that you have stomached the idea of unknowingly choosing this type of partner, this is where your work begins to consciously choose the partner that is best for you. I have often expressed on my YouTube channel titled: Mama Jr., that I am an advocate for counseling. On this channel, I talk about relationship matters and give advice to those who have sent in questions via email. In addition to therapy, you can also look into using other tools to help you discover how to avoid dating those same individuals that keep you going back to the dating pool. A vision board is a simple way to start! It will help you actually visualize your desires. There is no right or wrong way to put your board together because it's *your* vision! You can use a poster board, a cork board, white board or an empty wall in your house! As long as you write down and/or use pictures and other visual tools to keep you focused and motivated on your intentions, any way you put your board together is absolutely correct. A life coach may also be a means of supporting you with your relationship issues. While there are some similarities between a therapist and a life coach, a life coach is someone who can be more flexible in the ways they are able to help. They will also help you to identify your goals. They will also motivate and support you on the journey to accomplishing those things. They will hold you accountable to do the things you said you were going to do, and just like a coach, cheer you on every step of the way!

Now, while you are single, you should be coming to terms with what your deal-breakers are. (In fact, even if you are in a relationship, you would benefit from understanding what these are for you. Knowing this may or may not change your current relationship, but you owe it to yourself to always be honest with yourself in order to be honest with your mate.)

Once you have evaluated these things, finding and recognizing a potential partner will be easier. It'll also be easier to recognize who is *not* a potential partner. When you realize you don't want to date a person with certain qualities, you won't waste your time entertaining an individual who has those attributes. You can thank them for their interest and confidently say, "No, thank you." without second guessing yourself.

Understanding how to be successfully single means you are not desperate for a companion even though being in a relationship is one of your goals. My goals include having a personal chef and full-time masseuse, but I am not about to have just anyone come cook for me and I'm surely not about to let just anyone with hands come and rub me down! You see what I mean? Being true to your deal-breakers means you respect yourself and are not ashamed to say you are looking for a certain type of person. It means you are not hanging on to someone who is blatantly mistreating you or using you, or who is ungrateful for you all in the name of partnership.

Now, being true to your deal-breakers doesn't mean you're uptight or stuck up (even though you actually may be, but for the sake of this conversation, having standards doesn't put you in that category), it simply means you know yourself well enough to realize that you are not everyone's perfect mate nor will everyone be the perfect mate for you. This should make you feel good. Do you know how stressful it would be to keep second-guessing yourself, thinking maybe you should've been with someone else? Many people do it, thinking, *I should've just tried to get with such and such and maybe I would be better off.* Yeah, well, if you are paying attention to your deal breakers and respecting them, you'll realize you could not be more wrong about being with *such and such*.

So, let's talk about what you're doing with your single self. For starters, what do you enjoy doing alone? This is something to think about because, believe it or not, when you get into a relationship, you will have times when you absolutely need time to yourself. Trust me, it happens! If you are someone who doesn't like to be alone or doesn't like to do things alone, you need to figure out why. Think about it this way: you want someone to commit to being with you forever, but you don't like spending a few hours by yourself. What makes you think someone else will want to be with you, if *you* don't even want to be with you? Uh huh, now you're getting it!

Look, you may find a spouse before you finish reading this book, but you will still need to do some soul-searching. Being alone, does not mean you have to be lonely. While there is absolutely nothing wrong with preferring to be around others or preferring to spend your time with a partner, it would be nice if you learn to find equal enjoyment spending time with yourself. Think about it this way: you expect someone to see your awesomeness and, above all else, commit to being your partner for life through the covenant of marriage. You should be able to enjoy that same awesomeness while you are waiting to meet this person!

There are plenty of things you can do alone:

- You can enjoy your favorite restaurant alone. You might decide to eat at the bar or just get your food to go. If you do decide to stay, you don't have to feel bad about looking at your phone too much during dinner. You can eat as much as you want without trying to be courteous about the check and even order your favorite items to go!
- You can enjoy the movies alone, maybe that flick that your boo would never agree to see with you in a million years. You can sit wherever you'd like without having to be considerate of anyone else's seating preferences. You won't have to hear complaining about how dumb, scary, gross, girly or senseless the movie is. You'll just get to feel sheer

enjoyment watching the highly anticipated movie of your choosing! You can go at whatever time you'd like and it won't be an inconvenience to anyone else. Oh! And you can even dress in sweats because you are not trying to impress anyone. Ladies, I find when I'm dressed in sweats or looking messy from working around the house, this is when guys seem to be most interested for some reason. Go figure!

- You can enjoy travelling alone and you should! If you want to see any part of the world there is no reason you shouldn't. You should see the mountains, monuments and oceans of your choosing whenever you have the time and money to do so. Of course, whether you are alone or with someone, you should always plan these things safely and gain as much knowledge about the area and your lodging accommodations as you can, just to make sure you don't end up in a dangerous area. Also, make sure you are aware of necessary laws and customs if you are travelling out of the country.

We don't want you getting stuck overseas longer than you planned because you threw trash away in the wrong place! Once you have experienced all of these wonderful things, you can plan to go back and do these same things with your spouse and have new memories with him.

Now, even though I just made a compelling argument that would make some people think, *now tell me again why I should get married?* I am not trying to convince you to be single forever. I just want you to know there is a good side to being single and I want you to understand that you should enjoy your life no matter what your marital status is. There are always going to be things you'd rather do with someone else, but by *no* means should you be waiting on a partner to start living a fulfilled life. It is a very tall order to get with someone and expect them to be your everything. I mean, just think about that word: E V E R Y T H I N G. That's like being someone's parent. When a child is born, the parent has to be their everything. They have to decide what that child will eat and drink and what they will wear. They have to decide where the child goes, who they will or won't come into contact with, when to go to sleep and the list goes on and on. Do you really want your partner to be your everything? I don't, but if that's what you're looking for, I'm sure there is a controlling soul out there waiting to take over your life. Ultimately, though, you should complement your spouse, not be an empty vessel without them.

Next, let's talk about what you feel are your best traits that will internally and externally attract a mate. Now, this can be a very uncomfortable question for some people. I don't want you to feel like you need to go out and take up skydiving and get a face lift so you're more attractive. I want you to simply reflect. Think about that list of attributes that you want in your mate. Then, think... *What attributes will they be getting from me?*

While you are pondering this, I want you to be able to grow from the process. Part of that means you need to think about the things other people have said bothered them about you from other relationships. Now, this doesn't have to be feedback just from intimate relationships; it can be feedback that you've been given from family and friends as well. Have you been told you're selfish, not a good listener, disrespectful, self-centered, wasteful, ungrateful or other things? Whether you agreed with those things or wanted to hear them out at the time, it is still worth evaluating whether or not you were demonstrating those behaviors. We can only get better when we check ourselves!

The things that come up when you think this through are some things to think about and work on, because chances are your new spouse isn't going to be thrilled about those qualities in you either. Your boo may love your stinkin' feet, but when they realize they stink all of the time… not so much! As you are reflecting, recognize whether you have any qualities you are unwilling to change, even though you know they are seen as negative. I ask you to do this because some people just don't want to be giving, caring, compassionate individuals. It is important to be completely honest with yourself about who you are and if you want (or even think it is necessary) to make certain changes. Being honest with yourself is non-negotiable! Embrace who you are. If you like the person you are, stop pretending that you are or will become some form of yourself that you know good and well you are not trying to be. People often lie about who they are when a relationship is fresh and new, but expect their mates to be just as happy with them when they show their true colors later in the relationship. That is not the person they signed up to be with! Please, just be yourself from the start. It will be easier on your partner and less exhausting for you to keep up with a facade. Working on any negative qualities you possess will always make for a better marriage, but the reality is there are thousands of selfish, greedy people who have been married for years. Whether their spouse is happy with them or not is another story; but these characteristics haven't made them leave the relationship, so obviously they are not always deal-breakers. On the other side of this, if you do notice certain things you want to work on, now is the time. Not because you are single, but because you are reading this book. The present time is always the best time to work on yourself. Any self-improvement you make before you get into a relationship will only be better for the relationship. Why not give your spouse the very best version of yourself? Why start your relationship being a broken mess if you don't have to? And if you are currently in a relationship, why continue being a mess if you can clean things up?

I will say again, therapy may be very helpful for you if you are serious about making some life changes and tapping into some much-needed healing. I think everyone could benefit from counseling whether it becomes an ongoing source of support or something we do at different times in our lives for different reasons. It allows for us to have insight and support from a source that is truly there for the betterment of our mental health. There are so many things that pull at our inner fabric on a daily basis that we all need to make sure our mental health is intact. Stress can only be seen as it begins to manifest. As far as cost for therapy, look into the benefits offered by your employer first. Many companies offer some form of benefits that will pay for a certain number of visits to a counselor per year. If that is not an option, search online for mental health assistance or free counseling services in your area. You may even go as far as contacting a counselor and asking what options they may know of to cover counseling and see if there are programs or referrals that they can direct you to.

As you begin the journey of self improvement, take small steps. Working on ourselves can be extremely overwhelming as we are attempting to chip away at behaviors that have been a part of us for many years. You didn't develop all of your hang-ups in one day, so you won't be able to get rid of them all in one day. Take your time and make sure the bad habits are truly out of your system. You may find that some of your behaviors have developed over time as coping mechanisms to deal with

I'm Knot Ready

other things you have witnessed or experienced. Some things may have come as a result of the environment you have been exposed to or the company you keep. For example, you may have a standing hair appointment every two weeks because that's what your friends used to do and you wanted to fit in. At the time it seemed harmless, but now you realize you could save that money because you keep your hair pulled up in a bun most of the time anyway! Some of the things you may want to change are not always about your character. Make a list of things you know are issues that you'd like to work on and tackle them one at a time.

If you are unsure or unaware of areas for improvement, ask a trusted family member or friend if they can tell you three things they think you could work on. However! Do not ask if you know you are too sensitive or will be too defensive to receive the critique. You ought to know yourself well enough to know whether feedback is going to sting or if it will be devastating for you, whether that feedback is that you are selfish, loud, moody, unreliable, dishonest, promiscuous or don't keep a clean house. If you can't handle the truth, *don't ask!* It is not fair to get upset and say, "Such and such said I was this or that" if you solicited the information from them. Remember, they did not come to you, you came to them! And some folks have been waiting a long time to let you know what they think about you, so make sure you're ready!

Now that you have survived this soul-searching process of admitting you may have had a hand in your break-ups (and are working on it), you've realized there is happiness to be found in chilling by yourself, and have made peace with the notion of wanting to date someone like your dad... one could say that you are now, *successfully single!* CONGRATULATIONS!!!

Successfully Single

I Corinthians Chapter 7

32 I would like you to be free from concern. An unmarried man is concerned about the Lord's affairs—how he can please the Lord. **33** But a married man is concerned about the affairs of this world—how he can please his wife— **34** and his interests are divided. An unmarried woman or virgin is concerned about the Lord's affairs: Her aim is to be devoted to the Lord in both body and spirit. But a married woman is concerned about the affairs of this world—how she can please her husband. **35** I am saying this for your own good, not to restrict you, but that you may live in a right way in undivided devotion to the Lord. (NIV)

Chapter One Reflection

1. How I felt about being single before reading this chapter:

   _____
   _____
   _____

2. How I feel about being single now:

   _____
   _____
   _____

3. I have to admit I need to work on:

   _____
   _____
   _____

4. Things I am proud to be doing well:

   _____
   _____
   _____

Chapter 2

Know Why You Even Want To Be Married

So, what's the point? I mean why do you want to be married, anyway? Have you asked yourself these questions? Have you answered them? Are you comfortable with and proud of your answers? I ask this because not many people want to talk about why they want to be married in the first place. I mean, every consenting adult should just be able to get married if they so choose, right? Well, sure, but when talking about getting married, there really should be more of a reason other than, "because I want to." For the people who really want to be married, we know that they are anxious to do it, but we don't really ask why. When you think about marriage what comes to your mind? Don't give the "correct" answer that you expect should be said. For most people the first thought is of the wedding. If that's where your mind goes most times when you think of marriage, go ahead and admit it to yourself. Look, I completely understand the mind shift that takes you to envision this beautifully decorated venue surrounded by your family, friends and co-workers. I understand if you can't help but think of yourself and your betrothed, dressed to the nines, standing alongside bridesmaids and groomsmen with matching attire. I know what it's like to fantasize about how good you'll look during the traditional photo shoot and how happy you'll feel during the dances to your favorite romantic songs. I understand if you're already dreaming about those toasts that will make everyone cry. I know you will enjoy every moment with your hand in his when you cut the most amazing confection we all imagine to be included at the perfect wedding. Aww, I got you excited didn't I? WELL, SNAP OUT OF IT, TOOTS! The wedding is not the marriage. It is the first *day* of the marriage. Some folks get stuck on repeat thinking of the perfect wedding. It is only one day out of the rest of your life with this person. Focusing on the wedding is like focusing on having your first child or buying a house and expecting those specific events to represent married life. It is one of the many days you will spend with your spouse and you cannot possibly expect it to represent what life will be like with this person.

What about those of you thinking about marriage because "it's just time", "everyone else is doing it" or "I don't want to be by myself forever?" Let me just say that those are terrible reasons to make a covenant with another person before God.

Yes, there are right and wrong reasons to get married. Let's look at some examples that we have all heard or said at one point or another.

- "Because we've been together this long and may as well." NOPE!
- "Because I need financial security." TRY AGAIN!

- "Because they will leave me if I don't marry them." UNH UNH!
- "Because we have children together." HONEY PLEASE!

If any of the above reasons are your reason for wanting to get married, go back to the drawing board. Please do not insult your significant other by telling them any of those reasons are why you want to spend the rest of your life with them. Marriage is for keeps—or at least, it should be entered with that intent.

Marriage was created by God. The bible explains who should be married, how and why. It also explains situations in which the two are able to be separated and no, it is not only by death. The bible explains adultery and separating from a non-believer as reasons for divorce. Marriage is a covenant. It is probably the most important decision you will ever make in your life and should not be seen as something to do because, "it's just time." How insulting!

I'm Knot Ready

Marriage should be discussed and entertained as a commitment that two people are willing to make with one another because it will be pleasing to God and because they would like to build a family and want to show physical intimacy with one another without it being a sin. Marriage should be a decision you make after very careful consideration, after you are sure you are ready to commit your life to being the blessing that God has asked you to be in your potential spouse's life. See, you marrying this person is not about them *or* you getting what you want. Marriage is about God, or at least it should be. We know folks get married all the time and don't mention God one time after the ceremony is over, but that's another conversation. Marriage is about building with this person and protecting them as God sees fit. It is about demonstrating the love for one another that God has for the church.

Mama Jr.

In the book of 1 Corinthians, the Bible talks about the single person's intention being on God. So, if you don't want to be married, that's fine, because God wants all of your attention focused on Him anyway! When you think of marriage as it was intended, you will not haphazardly agree to become married because "everyone else is doing it." You are committing to be with this person, "in good times and bad times," "in sickness and in health," and "for as long as you both shall live," as the vows say. Now, since I spoke of the Bible, I feel I must mention that I am well aware the traditional wedding vows are not found in the Bible, but they do come from biblical principles. The reason for the vows is to remind you of the covenant between you, your spouse and God and therefore, should not be entered into by either person for superficial, self-serving reasons. Uncomfortable yet? Good. If we are going to talk about marriage, then we need to keep it all the way real. I would be doing you a great disservice if I simply told you what

I'm Knot Ready

you wanted to hear or focused on keeping it light and funny. It has to be the whole kit and caboodle! (Not familiar with "kit and caboodle?" Look it up... I told you, I'd show my age throughout this book!)

I felt that it was important to redirect your mind from the wedding because, guess what ladies? Most men don't give a rip about a wedding. Many men see it as an expensive waste of time. If they needed to throw a party to celebrate something it surely wouldn't include formally mailed invitations, flowers and a seating chart. They would have no problem going before a judge and just having a nice honeymoon on an island somewhere. I said "most" and "many" because obviously every man is not alike and some really do look forward to the wedding day. However, while more women than men daydream about that first glamorous day, men tend to focus on the responsibilities and restrictions that come with marriage. The reason that it tends to be so hard to get some men to agree to marriage is because some of them are not ready for the responsibilities of taking care of a family, a home, and all of the new restrictions that disallow them to hang out when and how they want (and more importantly *with whom* they want). There it is in a nutshell ladies! Your man is thinking about how he will provide for you. He is thinking about how he will provide for the children when they come. He is thinking about you telling him he needs to come home before a certain hour. He is thinking about you telling him what his priorities should or should not be. He is thinking about you telling him not to hang out with his one friend who attracts all of the single women. He is thinking about not being free to date whomever he wants because he is in a lifelong commitment with you. And, to be fair, depending on your relationship, those just might be valid, justifiable concerns.

We have to be honest about what marriage is and what it is not. Your marriage will not be like your parents', your friends', siblings', co-workers', and surely not like the scripted ones on television. Your marriage will be unique because it will be the only union that includes the two of you. No matter how similar another couple might be, they are not you and your spouse. Their lives began differently; they come from different families, their start as a couple and the things they have experienced as a couple will be different. They have different expectations and intentions for their marriage. They are simply not you. You need to think about this because folks often say, "I want a marriage like theirs. They have so much fun together," or, "They have been married for thirty years! I want a marriage like theirs." It is absolutely fine to want a marriage that is filled with laughter and lasts forever, but it will not— and I repeat, it will *not* be like anyone else's.

Often, you hear married people say that marriage is hard. I know I used to be confused by hearing this because I thought, *If we love one another enough to get married (which is the hard part), what could be hard about it?* HA! No, I should have said, HA, HA, HA, HA HA!!! Boy, oh boy! I hadn't the slightest idea!

Let's be clear: when I was a child, that unrealistic image of marriage was not painted by the people around me. I was mesmerized by the television version of marriage. My mother was not married, but my father was and I surely did not want a marriage like his and my stepmother's. My dad was hardly ever around. Even when I would ask to come spend a weekend with them, he'd tell me, "You can come over, but I won't be there." The time I spent at "my daddy's house" was with my stepmom and stepsister. That's just how it was. My dad would come home at night once we were asleep and had been out shopping or visiting with my stepmom's friends. We didn't do anything with him unless we went out of town to visit relatives, and even then, it was more visiting with relatives than anything else.

I'm Knot Ready

I didn't see my dad and stepmom hugging and kissing nor did I hear sweet comments made. I heard about some of the problems they had through a second party, but I didn't witness any of it myself. Some of my great aunts and uncles were married until they were parted by death and I have other aunts and uncles who have been married for more than forty years, but I didn't spend enough time to witness some grandiose example that would make me think marriage was not hard.

I take full responsibility for the fact that my misconception was created by myself, thanks to my favorite television shows and movies. Even as a teenager, I would fantasize about being married to whatever knuckle-headed boy I liked at the time. I daydreamed about how we would get into some argument that hurt my feelings and he would buy me flowers and snuggle up to me from behind. Oh yes, I had marriage all figured out chile! That is...until I got married.

I will start by saying this. I do not regret getting married. I was proud to be a wife, but it was not until the last year of my marriage that I truly focused on the purpose: to please God. I had finally realized why married people often said marriage was hard. Simply... because it involves another person! You cannot *ever* anticipate what another person will or won't do. You cannot script these things. And another person will almost *never* fulfill all of your needs. If you expect them to, please reread Chapter 1. *Do not pass go. Do not collect $200.*

Look, the person you marry has committed to be with you for the rest of their life. They felt sure they would have no problems keeping that commitment. But some of the things married people go through just can not be anticipated no matter how much the two of you plan. Your new spouse can't anticipate whether a month after you're married they will be offered a job in another state that would take you far away from everything you know and love...and that they

I'm Knot Ready

might want to take it! They can't tell you they might get sick and be out of work for a substantial amount of time and that the financial responsibilities will fall on you until whenever. They can't tell you if they will change their mind about wanting kids. They can't tell you if they are going to gain or lose a substantial amount of weight over the next ten years. They can't tell you how their looks will change. They can't tell you if they will forget an important date that marks a certain birthday or anniversary. They can't tell you if they'll develop a shopping habit that they won't see as an addiction, even if it puts you both in debt. They can't tell you if they'll start spending six hours a day playing video games, and that it won't just be a phase. They can't tell you they might become extremely attracted to a new co-worker and that, during a business trip, things may go a little too far. They can't tell you whether, after experiencing some tough times, they will start abusing drugs or alcohol. They can't tell you if family drama will create problems in your marriage. They can't tell you if they will suffer from depression after you've been married for thirty years. They can't tell you if their business venture will fail and cause a strain on your finances.

Whew! Before you ask, *no*, these are not examples from my marriage. I was only married for four years!

However, this is what you are signing up for when you say you want to be married: the unexpected. You are signing up to deal with the highs and lows that life gives to everyone, except you will be teamed up with someone as they happen. And that person may not be a fighter. You may have to carry certain burdens alone for one reason or another.

While I know I may have painted a gloomy picture of what marriage can be, obviously this is not destined to be *your* experience. Many of these examples can be avoided or handled well if you have good communication and a strong foundation when you begin your journey together. The people getting married because "everybody else is doing it", might not make it through these types of hurdles. They won't feel as if it is worth it because they didn't get married for the right reasons. Remember, marriage is a covenant, not a convenience. But for the people getting married with the right intentions; they will hopefully be able to batten down the hatches and come out of their storms stronger as a couple when faced with adversity.

Of course, there are many relationships that may absolutely negate these statements. The couple who got married for shallow reasons may grow as a couple and be stronger than anyone could have ever imagined, and the couple who seemed to have it all together could break up after year one. I simply want to help you understand why marriage can be hard and what it truly entails in order for you to approach the subject realistically and be as prepared as possible. Please don't get me wrong, your marriage will yield some beautiful memories. I pray the good ones easily outweigh the bad, but there will be challenges in every marriage, and if you are stuck with a fairy-tale expectation like I was as a teenager, you may end up a confused, divorced adult like I was as well.

Know Why You Even Want To Be Married

Proverbs Chapter 31

10 A wife of noble character who can find? She is worth far more than rubies.

11 Her husband has full confidence in her and lacks nothing of value. **12** She brings him good, not harm, all the days of her life.

26 She speaks with wisdom, and faithful instruction is on her tongue. (NIV)

Proverbs Chapter 18

22 He who finds a wife finds what is good and receives favor from the Lord.(NIV)

Chapter Two Reflection

1. Why I want to be married:

   _____
   _____
   _____

2. Before reading this chapter, I didn't consider:

   _____
   _____
   _____

3. I have to admit I can work on:

   _____
   _____
   _____

4. I know I am ready for marriage because:

   _____
   _____
   _____

Chapter 3

Learn How To Date

Ok, ladies! You are now successfully single. You have done some soul-searching and are working on becoming the best version of yourself. You have given yourself a true assessment as to why you want to be married and are still interested. Whew! I'm glad you're still with me. You are closer to meeting your boo-to-be and becoming their better half. The next step is to start dating. Yes! You're ready!

Now, if you ask ten people what their understanding of dating is, it is very possible you will get ten different answers. If you look up the definition of dating on the internet, Wikipedia has a very long and specific definition. Please read it if you'd like. If your intent is to be married, dating is the process of spending personal time with different people in hopes to make a strong enough connection with one of them that will lead to marriage. *Period!* And yes, I said "different people." There should not be any exclusivity until you have met someone and agreed that you are looking for the same things and want to see one another monogamously as you continue to build towards marriage.

Also, understand *seeing* and *sleeping* are entirely different things. I do not believe you should sleep with the people you are dating. It is dangerous and gets your heart wrapped up into a person that truly may not make the cut. We all know people (or are the people) who have gotten their hearts wrapped up with someone because they became intimate too soon. We also know people who have had children with that person because they had sex before they figured out if they even really like that person. Now they have to be connected with this person for the next eighteen years and can't stand the sight of them! If you want to be married, you cannot afford to get caught up with the wrong people anymore. Get serious about your life— it's game time! You are looking for marriage, so make decisions with your head and not your crotch!

Most people are dating with a purpose. That purpose could be marriage, friendship or just sex. The problem is, many people fail to tell the person or people they are dating what that purpose is. Now, the omission of this information may be for a few different reasons.

1. They didn't realize they should be so direct so soon.

2. They don't want to scare the person off.

3. They simply do not *know* what their purpose is.

If you want to be married, your intent should be discussed on the first date. Yes, the very first. Now, you don't need to come in like a drill sergeant making a declaration on a bullhorn, "DO YOU WANT TO GET MARRIED OR ARE YOU LOOKING FOR A BOOTY CALL SOLDIER?!! SPEAK UP! THIS AIN'T A GAME MAGGOT!!!" That would surely leave you swatting away exhaust fumes, because this person is going to burn rubber speeding away from you! You do, however, need to be clear that you are looking for a meaningful relationship that will turn into something permanent and your goal is to be married.

What we often do in the beginning of relationships is give the new person an easy entrance. We like what we see and want to keep the new person around and convince them we are worth it, so we are afraid of saying the actual words that would express what we want. You will save yourself so much time if you are direct with the people you date. It is ok to let a "fine one" get away if the "fine one" is not the right one for you!

If you let them know you want to be married, they might just let you know they have vowed to *never* get married for one reason or another. If you encounter this person, respect them for being up front with you. If someone says they don't want to get married, *believe them*. Enjoy the rest of the date and let them know that while you had a nice time, you are looking for a person who wants the same things you want. Now, this is where you need to be strong! It won't always be that easy to just make this statement and be done. There is a strong possibility this person may say something to try to convince you to continue seeing them because of *their* intentions. "Well, as fine as you are *or* a beautiful smile like that might make me change my mind." Don't do it! They have already told you their truth. A cute face and a nice smile surely should not make them change a whole vow against being married. Unh Unh.

If you do decide to keep their number or go out again, they need to understand that you know *exactly* what you want and, because you do, you are seeing other people. Tell them this, please! You need people to take you seriously at this stage or you're going to keep playing games with players! They also need to know your *smile* is the only sunshine you will be providing because sex is not an option, and you absolutely need to mean this! Some people love a challenge and just want the opportunity to prove you wrong. I know you'd like to argue with me on this but you've done it your way in the past and you are still single. You've given in to too many "fine ones" and you have yet to send out wedding invitations. Just go ahead and admit that sex complicates things. It does not belong in the early stages of dating.

Look, just because they are fine, do you want to spend the next several years convincing them that you are worth it? I would surely hope not! If you give in to your charming dinner date now, they'll spend the next few years reminding you they already told you they didn't want to be married whenever you bring it up. You need to be equally yoked. You need to be with someone who has the same relationship goals you have, and there is nothing wrong with finding out what those goals are early on. It should be a standard you set. You can find out their favorite color and whether they are a dog person or cat person later. And if you do meet someone who shares your same goals at the beginning, definitely keep the lines of communication open throughout the relationship to know when and if those goals change. If they have changed, there needs to be communication about how to still be on the same page and make whatever compromises are necessary to remain happy and fulfilled within the relationship.

Let's talk about what you can do to get the most out of your dating experience beyond that first conversation. First of all, you need to think about your safety. For some it goes without saying, but others need to be reminded. Some of you can be too trusting or swayed by the preliminary conversations and interactions you've shared with certain people and then you let your guards down. Everyone does not have your same agenda! Everyone was not raised the way you were raised. Some people are deeply troubled and will not think twice about creating the opportunity to rob you, hurt you or kill you. There are plenty of people out there that can tell you these are real things that can happen on a "nice date with a nice person." When you are dating, "spending time with different people"… spend time with them in a public place. Going to a date's home or letting them come to yours leaves you vulnerable. One thing many people regret after a situation goes sour is letting that shady shyster know where they live. Yes, a long term relationship can also go bad, but you want to limit how many people have access to the place you are supposed to have peace.

Sometimes, we choose people just because they chose us, simple as that. Let me tell you here and now, *that is not how to choose a partner!* You are *way* better than that. You don't need to accept the first person who comes your way simply because they chose to have a conversation with you. There needs to be a strong level of discernment applied when it comes to allowing someone to become a part of your life. Very few people deserve access to your heart and it's time to start acting like it. Some of us are not used to having people interested in us, which gives the first person who expresses interest an all-access pass. Well, not anymore! There must come a time in your life when you realize that, while you may not have ever been an internet

I'm Knot Ready

hottie, you are an amazing individual because being you is enough. Maybe *not* knowing this about yourself is the reason that certain undesirables come your way! I am not saying that your past relationships were with scum (and maybe they were, let's just keep it real), but if past partners treated you badly and did so unapologetically, you need to realize they saw something in you that made them feel like they could. The way you treat yourself tells others how they can treat you. Once past partners crossed the line and you didn't address it (or maybe you did but you stayed in the relationship), they learned a little about what they could get away with. They learned what apologies worked, if they needed to be pitiful looking or even pop out a few tears. They learned to use their previous traumas as excuses as to why they lash out a certain way or say you're the only one who understands them. They learned they could manipulate you by reminding you of how they've been abandoned in the past and how they couldn't take another person rejecting them. I've even known some to use the ultimate form of manipulation and threaten to kill themselves (or you) if you leave them. And I am not saying this threat is only manipulation because some people have carried out these statements.

Disclaimer: If you are currently in a relationship with someone who has threatened to kill themselves or you under any circumstances, you need to call the police to intervene. It is not up to you to battle with someone who has these types of problems, and while they may have made these threats in vain in the past, you don't know when and if the day will come where they actually will make good on those threats.

These are all examples of toxic relationships and hopefully you are no longer involved in situations like this because you're single. Some people have no shame or restrictions about how far they are willing to go to manipulate and control you.

Another reason some of you are not having success in your relationships is because you are simply choosing partners

I'm Knot Ready

for selfish, shallow reasons. If you choose a partner solely based on their wealth, what do you do when you find out that they don't like to share? You're single again. What do you do when they ask you to sign a prenuptial agreement? You're single again. What do you do when they explain the only way you can have access to their money is to do deplorable, degrading things? Hopefully, you're single again. I say that because no dollar amount is worth your dignity. Letting someone treat you like dirt is not worth any amount of money, ever! You may ask why and I'll tell you like my mother used to tell me, because I said so. Now get it together!

You need to think about what you want in a spouse. I'm going to keep using that word, "spouse", because you are not just looking for a good time with someone. You are looking for your spouse, and you need to program your mind to start admitting that. It is ok to say it to yourself and tell others the same thing. You don't want to waste time kicking it and hanging out for years. You can Netflix and chill in the home you share with your spouse, while sipping the wine they bought, while admiring the ring on your left hand, while they're rubbing your feet on the couch you two bought...

Oh, wait. I went off on a tangent there. Now, what was I saying? Oh, yeah! Think about what you want. Now, many people will tell you things didn't work out with an individual because they just weren't their type. When people say this, people are usually talking about physical attributes. If this is what has stopped you from dating someone or getting to know a person, this is a new day. Who cares about your type?! When we think about what our "type" is, a certain celebrity comes to mind. Well, let me tell you something sweetheart: most of those people are taken! They are not able to be a husband to the millions of people that are attracted to them, and often their looks and fame are all they have going for them because they are a mess to deal with in real life. You need to start digging deeper than dimples and muscles and look at what will make a great spouse for you. Does your ideal partner really have to be a dead ringer for your favorite celebrity crush? If so, please reread Chapter 1. *Do not pass go. Do not collect $200.*

Now, I think I am a pretty good catch for several reasons, but I am so glad that my boo didn't say, " A woman who wears glasses, has a crooked tooth and is shorter than 5'5" is not my type", or he would've passed me up. I'm not saying that dating you should be a free-for-all, but you must be realistic that there are no perfect people. The man or woman you are looking for with a certain skin tone, hair texture, body type, college degree and sexual prowess might just not be on the dating website of your choosing right now. If they are, you need to understand that those are not the only characteristics that they bring to the table. Have you ever seen an intelligent man who couldn't buy himself a sense of humor? Or maybe he earned a lot of money but had nothing to show for it! Honey, let me tell you… I have! I know that we want it all, but you need to think about what you are really willing to compromise in order to meet your list of standards. I'm not trying to discourage you from finding what you want, but be realistic. If you believe your spouse will come in the package that you desire, they just surely might. Keep hope alive! But keep in mind you may find the love of your life in the person who didn't go to college but is still very ambitious and successful. It may surprise you that your perfect mate doesn't have a beach body, but they eat right, exercise regularly and are very healthy. I don't want you to go out with someone whom you just can't stomach, but I do believe you can find love in the most unexpected places. Oh, and just remember… you might not check off all of the boxes on someone else's list either, but they still chose to get to know you.

While you are getting to know this person or these people, pay attention to their actions. Please don't invest all of your time grinning and blushing like an idiot while they are putting up huge red flags. Dating should be an interview process, my dear, and you need to check out every little thing you can in order to pick the right person for the job! Make sure their actions line up with the things they are telling you. If the things they are telling you don't make sense or contradict things they have previously said or done, call them out on it. It doesn't have to be an argument. It *shouldn't* be an argument. You don't have to have a knock-down, drag-out fight because you caught them in a lie, but they must know you will not take their foolishness at any point. They need to know early on being in your life at any stage requires honesty.

Remember, you are only dating and this is when the benefits of abstaining from sex pays off. Realizing they are not what they seem might be a deal-breaker for you, and cutting them off will be that much easier if you haven't been playing house. Dating is the part of your journey where you learn this individual and are possibly building a foundation. This is where you decide if this person is trustworthy and then make the appropriate decisions accordingly. Now, if they lied once… you already know! You are *not* desperate. You do *not* need to set up shop with a person who is dishonest for any reason. And if you are having a hard time breaking it off with a person at this stage because you're too nice, you don't want to hurt their feelings or you think that you might be able to change them, do me a favor and reread Chapter 1. *Do not pass go. Do not collect $200.* You might not be strong enough for this part of the process yet, because the sharks are going to eat you alive. They unapologetically want to meet a trusting, easy to manipulate soul that cannot stand up for themselves. Just saying!

Lastly, let's think about how you put yourself out there in the dating pool. If you are dating online, you need to create a true representation of yourself. Please don't put a bunch of pictures up of yourself from eighty pounds ago! We get it, those are more flattering pictures, but baby, that is not who your date is going to meet next week when you go out! Let them know what you look like *today*. Be proud of who you are, there is no shame in being you! Be honest in your bio. Make sure you are clear about your intentions to avoid any undesirables.

When you go out, dress with class. Your breast and behind should not be hanging out. You are trying to become a wife. There is honor in that. You don't have to wear a turtleneck (unless "Old Man Winter" is nipping), but leave something to the imagination. If you are pulling and tugging at your outfit, wear something else, plain and simple. I know you love the design and the color looks great on you but you need to be comfortable. You know you've seen the female whose skirt was so short it was brushing her crotch. She kept pulling and tugging at the sides of it every few minutes. We all sit and think, *why did you wear it in the first place if you knew it didn't fit?!* Ladies, men love a confident woman. If you are self-conscious about what you are wearing and how you look, it will show. Also, most men do not want other men checking their woman out. A glance or so, maybe, but men don't want other dudes

Mama Jr.

gawking at the woman he's with because they hope a nipple will pop out at any moment. Also, the kind of husband you are looking for won't be attracted to the kind of woman who thinks she has to try that hard! They know you have breasts, legs and thighs. They don't need a reminder over dinner.

Also, think about your hygiene. There's no quicker way to turn a man off than having an odor coming from you! Make sure you smell nice, but don't overdo the perfume. Just bathe! If you have *any* hair on your face, go have it waxed or pluck it yourself. By the way, this is a hard fast rule whether or not you go on another date for the rest of your life!

Make sure you don't have any visitors in your nose, either. Brush thoroughly and swish around some mouthwash. Even though you do the last two, old food between your teeth can make for a bad, bad date, so make sure you floss! Iron your clothes. If they are new, you should have washed them first, but if you didn't make sure they don't have fold marks and creases in them.

Don't overdo the makeup unless that's your daily thing. Your date wants to be able to recognize you the next time he sees you! On the other hand, if you are not a makeup person, that's fine but put something on your lips, even if it is only Chapstick. Make sure your lips are not dry and crusty.

Wear shoes that are comfortable to walk in and, if you really and truly want this thing to work, do not wear an open-toed shoe or expose your heals without a recent pedicure. I cannot tell you how bad some of these feet are out here, chile!

Lastly, make sure your hair is on point. You don't have to get it done the day of, but make sure it looks nice however you decide to style it. Take a comb or brush to clean up any flyaway hairs and make sure a random gust of wind doesn't leave you looking like a charity case.

Hopefully, this helps you think about dating differently and you can note some things you haven't been doing and will plan on doing when you are ready for dating. I'm so excited about the progress you are about to make and the time you surely will not waste entertaining losers.

Learn How to Date

I Corinthians Chapter 7

8 Now to the unmarried and the widows I say: It is good for them to stay unmarried, as I do. **9** But if they cannot control themselves, they should marry, for it is better to marry than to burn with passion. (NIV)

Chapter Three Reflection

1. How I feel about dating:

   _____
   _____
   _____

2. This chapter has revealed:

   _____
   _____
   _____

3. I'll have to admit that I need to work on:

   _____
   _____
   _____

4. How I know I am ready to date:

   _____
   _____
   _____

Chapter 4

Is Your Steady Ready?

Ok, so when you've found someone to become exclusive with hopefully your dating days will be over! If you are already dating exclusively, Congratulations! Being in an exclusive relationship is a great thing and it's one more step closer to marriage. I know it was hard to identify your shortcomings and work on them, but you did it and are better for it! Also, it must've been frustrating to have dated people who constantly missed the mark. I know it felt like you were never going to meet anyone worthy of a lifelong commitment, but GLORY TO GOD!!! You found the one you didn't want to let get away and now you are learning more about each other every day. This is such a good thing. Now is the time for you two to establish the foundation of your relationship.

Mama Jr.

I know it would be nice to just admire how good they look and remind yourself of how great your taste in the opposite sex is, but let's do things differently so this time is for keeps, because you really do want to be married and this person seems to have great potential.

I know it may seem like you have put in a lot of work just to connect with your potential spouse and this is exactly what you're doing. This is what you need to get used to because marriage is work. You are attempting to join your life with another person. That is not an easy task. I know the movies and television shows have led us to believe that it will be effortless if only you love one another, but do not be deceived my friend! Committing to someone for the rest of your life is no easy feat. You are telling yourself you are capable of making a decision now that you are willing to stand by forever. Most people can't even commit to a hairstyle, a career path, or where they want to live! How could committing to a whole person be any easier? Your

I'm Knot Ready

potential spouse is coming to the relationship with their own mindset about life, and while theirs might very well mesh perfectly with your mindset, it will and can vary depending on the topic or scenario. People can't say how they will respond to every life situation, which makes it that much more difficult to know if you can trust them as your partner. This is why the beginning of your relationship should be used to set the foundation of what your relationship together will look like. This is the time to establish the trust, loyalty and integrity you can expect from one another. This is the time for you to learn how they deal with the issues that will inevitably come up in life and affect you both. You need to pay attention to how they deal with money, family, career, friends, children and other responsibilities.

We like to say this or that is "not my business, we're not married." But wouldn't you like to know before you get married if the love of your life has gambling debts in the six figures and their income is in the very low five figures? Wouldn't you like to know if they have no intention of advancing within their career or having children with you? Wouldn't you like to know if they are willing to invest all of their money and yours on get-rich-quick schemes because "you only live once?" Do you think it would be beneficial to know if they use recreational drugs and if they have been in and out of rehab for years?

I know these things sound extreme, but people deal with these and even more bizarre things every day. You'd better believe that they wished they would have learned this information before saying, "I do!" The point I am trying to make is people waste the beginning of their relationships learning trivial, superficial information and the necessary information doesn't come along until after they have signed the marriage license.

Personally, I would like to know if my man has ever been physically violent towards their partner. I want to know if he is financially stable and gainfully employed and what habits he has (simple or serious). I could go on and on, but you get the gist, (I hope).

Now, please keep in mind the efforts you put into this person may be one-sided. If they are not serious about putting in the work, your relationship could fail. However, it will only be a benefit to you to learn the type of person your potential partner is and decide if you will continue to invest in them or move on. This is the part of the relationship that allows you to determine if this person is truly the one that you were meant to spend your life with. You should be getting to know them. You should be learning their quirks, pet peeves and those little idiosyncrasies that are so cute they just make you love your boo more and more. But let's be real. You'll be learning some things that will make you wanna snap their neck and if they keep up with those annoying behaviors that is exactly what's going to happen! *Sigh* But on a serious note, this is the time in your relationship that allows you to set the tone for the rest of your relationship. You get to demonstrate your true self and hopefully get to see theirs. You get to see how they interact with their family and friends and how they interact with yours. You get to determine if they really do know how to treat you well and whether or not they have some things to work on in that area. You get to have those important conversations that will allow you to see where their maturity level is and if they can really keep up with where you are in life. Along the way, you will speak about each other's goals and aspirations for career and family and if this person is a winner, their goals will match up with yours. But what do you do when their goals don't exactly match up with what you want? What do you do when this particularly important conversation comes up and you've been dating close to (or over) a year? You have fallen in love and there are so many things that you appreciate and respect about this person, but in this area of conversation, their views could not be more different than yours. Well, this is where the adult in you kicks in. You need to realize this is where you keep talking to gain some clarity on how set they are as it pertains to the subject matter. For example if your partner says they do not want to have children, you need to find out if they mean "at this time in their life" or *ever*. Also, you need to be clear about your own position with this subject. If you want children now or are not sure, this needs to be a conversation that you two have until you have no more questions left and you both are 100% sure you understand the other person's position. This conversation and the ones that follow should not be an attempt to convince or persuade them to change their mind. However, you surely need to keep the dialogue going until you know exactly how they feel and why. Often we get upset, offended and defeated when our partner does not share our life goals, but their position on certain topics may make perfect sense to you once you hear them out.

You may even respect their position enough to change your stance! Again, changing one another's minds is not the goal of having these conversations, but it is not fair to dismiss them or be angry with them just because they don't arrive at the conversation with the same mindset as you. This, my friend, is what marriage is going to be about on many days: having hard conversations and coming up with some semblance of a compromise. Be clear, however, that a compromise does not mean both of you are going to walk away by getting some of what you want. When talking about kids, you both may decide not to have your own, but to adopt instead—or you might decide that you are *not* going to start a family, a decision that could cause a new set of issues, resentment being one of them.

So how do you have this conversation and not have resentment when the other person is not budging on their stance? Respect the fact that your partner is entitled to feel the way they feel just as you do. Respect the fact they were mature enough to tell you their truth, even though it doesn't match yours. Remember this is not your relationship, alone. This is a relationship that the two of you share. You don't want your partner harassing you and becoming disgruntled because of how you feel, so don't do that to them. When you have talked everything out and have learned their reasons for feeling how they feel, you both have a decision to make: ***Stay or Leave.***

Your heart just skipped a beat, didn't it? I know, I know! You have gone through so much to find this person and the thought of not moving forward with them is too much to bear. We've reached grown folks status here, my dear, and we have to talk about it. But know that I don't want you to be in an unhealthy relationship. If you are being denied children within your relationship and you feel very passionately about it, this will be unhealthy. The same goes for the person who does not want children and is being forced to start a family: that's unhealthy too. We all know

Mama Jr.

people who stayed together even though they could not agree on whether or not to have kids. When they have kids to make one person happy, the other one uses every opportunity to remind everybody they didn't want kids anyway! With the other situation, when one person is deprived of having the child or children they long for, they constantly tell people how much better their life would be if they had a family of their own. Why do that to yourself? Now, don't get me wrong, I am not saying that you should necessarily end a relationship if the person you are with doesn't agree with you on major things such as whether or not to have kids. What I *am* saying is if you feel strongly about a topic and your partner has an opposing view, then unhappiness could ensue. On the matter of having children, I would say you two should truly be on the same page. If you aren't and intend to stay in the relationship, you may need to seek counseling to further discuss some options on how to make peace with the fact that someone is not going to get what they want.

I remember being in a long distance relationship when I was around twenty-six or twenty-seven years old. He was in Illinois; I was in Michigan. I was visiting family when I met him and we agreed that we would make the drive to visit one another. We dated for about three or four months. Long story short, he had a daughter already. He focused on how expensive it was and he was adamant that he didn't want any more children. My thinking was he didn't know what he wanted and once he got to know me better, he'd be begging me to marry him and have a child. Well, um...no! While we'd grown fond of one another, the subject kept coming up and he finally let me know he didn't want to keep me from the man I was supposed to be with. He said he was sure he did not want any more children and he was not going to change his mind. I heard him out and thanked him for being honest and we wished each other well. I cried for a few minutes when we hung up the phone, and then I moved on. I knew the breakup was for the best and I was glad he was able to do what I couldn't do at that time. These are the types of decisions that you may have to make. Sure, nothing like this comes up in our fairy-tale daydreams. The toughest decisions we make in our daydreams are about which china pattern to buy! (There I go showing my age again. Does anyone choose china patterns anymore?) Anyway, while it may be a painful blow to let a good one get away, it might actually be the decision you need to make when it comes to doing what is best for you. And while deciding on whether or not to have children could be a difficult discussion, what do you do when your boo doesn't want to get married?

Well, marriage *is* the reason for this book, right? I mean, you want to be married, right? Well, it is very possible that the one you found after sifting through many hopefuls just doesn't want to be married.

I'm Knot Ready

Now, the truth is, you may have had this conversation in the beginning and, when you did, they told you what you wanted to hear. OR! They did not lie to you, but instead, they have truly changed their mind. OR! They told you they didn't want to get married at the beginning, still don't want to be married and you are just now realizing after being with them this long…they meant it.

Boy, oh boy! You're in a pickle now.

Look, I could have inserted some statistics here about how many couples live together for however many years without ever getting married. But what's the point? Either you know several people who once did or are currently living this way, or you are involved in cohabitation yourself. What you need to know is that it happens and, if you aren't careful, you will be among the many and marriage will be just as far away as it's ever been.

So, why do people prefer this way over getting married? I mean, these people don't seem to be just passing through.

Mama Jr.

They have bought houses and had children together. They have bills together and have been through the good and the bad. So, why aren't they married?

My question is why should they be? They are living the married life with all of the things described above. Why would you want to be married when you already have the security of knowing that bae is obviously not going anywhere after all of your time together?

I can't and won't attempt to answer for the countless couples who have chosen this way to live. It must be working for them. I am not going to tell them they should all go down to the courthouse and have a judge declare them married. I will say though, it is not an option for me, and since you're reading this book, it obviously is not for you.

Before I was married, my ex-husband and I lived together for a year. I had never lived with a partner before him and I have not cohabitated since. While I think it was a great way

I'm Knot Ready

to learn about one another, I did feel guilty about us not being married before living together. Thinking back, I realize that I learned things about him that should have helped me to realize we were not ready for marriage, but my wanting to be married overshadowed the notes I should have been taking. We were having sex right out of the gate, (I mean that's what you do when you live together, right?) so we were playing house and had not really discussed the important things that would've been necessary to make wiser decisions. He was divorced with two children and at one point told me he had too much baggage and wasn't ready for another marriage. At the time, I felt like I heard him, but we were already living together by this point and he wasn't exactly moving out as he said this. So what did I do? I wrote him a long letter that basically said we could live together because I didn't think it was fair to put him out, but we would not be having sex anymore. I knew I had put the cart before the horse, but I had to try to get this thing right at some point. I also explained that while it might feel like it, my letter was in no way meant as an ultimatum. I didn't want him to feel forced or settle for me. I really wanted to be chosen and I didn't want him to marry me for sex, I was more than that.

Well, after three or four months of being roommates he told me he wanted to be married. Do you think I argued? *Nope!* I was flattered and foolish all at once. He took my desperation to be a wife and I gladly took his name for all it was worth—until after four years we called it quits.

I don't go into much detail about my ex-husband here because there are two sides to a story. I respect his side and won't put him in a position to defend it. It's listed as a point of reference to help you, but he and I have been divorced longer than we were married to one another and I refuse to bash him or air our dirty laundry to sell a book.

Now, like I said earlier, either a person can tell you what you want to hear, change their mind, or tell you the truth from the start, even as you choose to ignore it. As you can see, I went through all of the above. Now, I am not saying my ex-husband never wanted to be married. I can assume he wanted to since he did it, but the truth is, we never really had that discussion. I know he did tell me his truth, and also that he did eventually tell me what I wanted to hear. He may have been happily married to me (I'd like to believe he was) but it wouldn't surprise me if he were to say it happened sooner than he'd liked it to.

This is where you get to learn from the choices I made, the choices the people around you have made, and the choices *you* have made in the past. You must communicate, my dear! No one should be forced into or settle for marriage! In Chapter 3, I spoke about this because you claim to be serious about getting married. You know the saying "closed mouths don't get fed?" Well, this is a good example. If you don't communicate your needs then you won't have them met. Plain as that. If your partner told you they don't want to get married for whatever reason, please, please, please believe them! It is perfectly fine to discuss their reasons if they are willing to share, but you must understand they can't tell you any more plainly. Your willful persistence to be married is not going to make your partner want to marry you. Once you hear them tell you their truth, you have a decision to make: ***Stay or Leave.*** If you stay, you are accepting their terms of not wanting what you want. If you leave, you choose to be single again and be available for the person who *does* want what you want.

Now, if you started this process like you were supposed to, putting your truth out there and accepting theirs, this decision should be an obvious one. You should already know your deal-breakers; so ideally, you won't be writing a letter advising of your new decision to withhold sex. However, if you *are* living with your partner and you are now sitting here with your eyes welling up, realizing that as long as you've been with your partner, as much as the two of you have been through, and as much as you love each other, they really don't want to get married... it's time to have a talk.

This talk may not be with your partner, yet. It may be with yourself, with a therapist, with God, or all of the above. Ending a relationship is not an easy decision. But neither is staying in a relationship where your needs aren't being met. We always want to make the best decisions without regrets, which is not easy to do. Maybe you need to go back to Chapter 2 and ask yourself why you want to be married anyway. What does it mean to stay with your partner without marriage? Will you be able to be happy? Will you wonder why you aren't "good enough"? Will you be concerned about the example you are setting for your child or children? Will you stay as you've seen others do, because if you try hard enough you can convince yourself marriage is only a piece of paper? Or would you be oddly satisfied without your partner if you end the relationship?

Would you find peace in knowing you did not settle for a situation that was not right for you?

I could go on and on with the questions, but only you can decide what will be best for you. I can say for me that I want to be married because my biggest goal in life is to please God. I want him to be proud of me and the decisions I make. I know God approves of marriage and if I want to be physical with a man and/or have a family, this is the way to go about it. I want to be married because there is respect and honor in being a "Mrs" and, if I am going to be on the arm of the man I love, I deserve the respect and benefits that come with him claiming me as his wife. I deserve to wear the ring of his choosing to symbolize that we have made a covenant respected by God. I deserve to have him leave his family and cleave to me. I deserve to be able to take care of him as the Lord wants and carry his name as we create a legacy to be admired for generations to come. I deserve marriage because I will no longer waste my time "kicking it" with someone who merely likes to have me around. No, ma'am.

I cannot speak for you. I can only speak for myself and as for me; I deserve marriage because it is a standard I have set for myself as a lady and a child of God.

Is Your Steady Ready?

I Corinthians Chapter 7

1 Now for the matters you wrote about: "It is good for a man not to have sexual relations with a woman." **2** But since sexual immorality is occurring, each man should have sexual relations with his own wife, and each woman with her own husband. **3** The husband should fulfill his marital duty to his wife, and likewise the wife to her husband. **4** The wife does not have authority over her own body but yields it to her husband. In the same way, the husband does not have authority over his own body but yields it to his wife. **5** Do not deprive each other except perhaps by mutual consent and for a time, so that you may devote yourselves to prayer. Then come together again so that Satan will not tempt you because of your lack of self-control. **6** I say this as a concession, not as a command. (NIV)

10 To the married I give this command (not I, but the Lord): A wife must not separate from her husband. **11** But if she does, she must remain unmarried or else be reconciled to her husband. And a husband must not divorce his wife. (NIV)

Chapter Four Reflection

1. How I felt about being in a relationship before reading this chapter:

   _____

   _____

   _____

2. What I now realize about being in a relationship:

   _____

   _____

   _____

3. I can admit I need to work on:

   _____

   _____

   _____

4. In my current relationship (or when I was in a relationship), I am (or was) doing these things well:

   _____

   _____

   _____

Chapter 5

Patience My Friend... Patience

I have a question for you (yes another one). Are you ready to be married? I know that is a weird question to ask someone halfway through a book they're reading about getting married, but I still pose the question. Are you ready to be married? As I referenced in the Introduction, *Married At First Sight* has become a consideration for some who are tired of trying to find the right one on their own. I'm sure that most could say that while it is interesting to watch, they don't have the nerve to marry a stranger. Most would agree that meeting Mr. or Mrs. right would still yield some "getting to know you time", so I ask you to remember this as you are eager to marry the one you may be with. One thing I want you to keep in mind is at this point (if you are in a relationship), is that your partner knows how you feel about marriage. You have communicated how you want to be married to them, why you'd like to be married and you'd like it to happen in whatever time frame you discussed. I presume this to be true because we talked about how important it is to be forthcoming about your intentions at the beginning of your relationship. If you have not been crystal clear about these things, *stop!!! Do not pass go! Do not collect $200!* We are not going to play the, "he should already know" game. If you have not said the words, "I want to be married to you within the next 2-4 years," don't expect your partner to know. Sure, they might (and it'd be great if they could read your mind), but communication is key and assuming, guessing, hoping and wishing is not going to ensure your needs are met in this relationship. Some people think, "they know I love them" means they know I want to marry them." *Uh, no!* Some folks will take a bullet for you and give you their last dime, but that has nothing to do with them wanting to be married. Look, you can play all of the games that Milton Bradley and Hasbro can make, but you better stop playing games when it comes to your relationships! Be clear, direct, honest and serious when it comes to matters of the heart or yours might be the next one to get broken.

Since you have communicated what you feel and they have communicated the same to you, be patient. Continue to strengthen your bond and get to truly know this person. A person is not going to show all of their character traits in one month. It takes time to see a person's temperament. It takes time to see how they interact with the people in their lives. It takes time to see how they manage their finances and other responsibilities. It takes time to see if they have a relationship with God and what that relationship looks like. You want to remember while you will always be growing and learning together (because the two of you will be constantly changing), some things are already woven into the fabric of this person. Their morals and values are already with them and only time will allow you to see how that coincides with *your* morals and values. If you can learn the depth of this person's character before you marry them, why wouldn't you?

There are some people out there who have many wonderful attributes about them but they are sneaky, deceitful, manipulative opportunists whose only true goal in life is to "come up" by any means. I don't want to be with someone like that. I don't want to be with someone whose integrity is for sale. I would choose being single for the rest of my life if my only choice for a mate was someone who is shadier than a palm tree. And this is just *my* point of view. Your choices may come from a different perspective based on some things you have seen or experienced in your life. The true nature of your partner is what I want you to take the time to observe as you decide whether or not to give them full access to your life. I know your goal is marriage and you feel like you've been waiting forever, but believe it or not, you have time to learn your potential spouse. You have time to make sure *this* decision is the *right* decision. Being patient during this time is also important because as you get to learn your partner, you will be able to identify their intentions. We have spoken about what you want and helping your partner understand your needs; but it is just as crucial for you to identify and understand *their* needs. If your mate needs more attention, validation, hugs and kisses than you are used to giving, it's important to know this now so you know how to adapt. These types of things speak to a person's love language and when a person doesn't hear their language being spoken, they can feel like they are not being loved. If this is going to be your spouse, you need to know how to love them.

One thing I pride myself on is being a good caretaker. I am a true nurturer and have been since I was a very small child. I simply find pleasure in taking care of people and knowing they are well because of my attentiveness to their

Mama Jr.

needs. Well, imagine my conundrum to have dated a guy that didn't appreciate my cooking! When I asked how a particular meal tasted, his reply was, "It's food. I don't care what it tastes like. I'd eat a rat if I were hungry enough." Needless to say we didn't make it! My food has never been five-star, but it is far from being compared to survival portions from a rat! We didn't break up because of food of course, but I should have known I would never make it with a man that couldn't appreciate my cooking. LOL! *but seriously*.

When you learn how to love a person, you learn what they need to feel safe, secure and at home with you. You learn to add peace to their lives. As their spouse, you should be a source of peace for them. As this happens, they learn to trust you, confide in you and depend on you. These are huge aspects because nowadays, folks have a hard time trusting others. They have been hurt so many times and have built concrete barriers around their hearts because of their pain. Only time will allow you to get emotionally close to someone who is afraid of being hurt.

I'm not saying you can only get married when you've accomplished this. Obviously, some people are dealing with deep issues that will take years of therapy to address. If you have demonstrated that you are consistent and honorable however, they may realize you are the one they can work through their pain with, so be patient.

On the other side of the coin, patience does not mean you need to be gullible. Let me be clear: folks will misuse you if you allow them to. It doesn't matter how open, honest, nice, genuine, patient or supportive you may be. If there is a way for them to get over on you, some people will do it. Your job during the "getting to know you" stage is to identify and weed those individuals out *quickly!* Maybe you're not astute enough to identify those people. Maybe you keep getting your heart broken because a player with the right line and a nice smile finds you each time. If that is

Mama Jr.

what you keep running into, that is where you need to start. Think about the things these people tend to get from you when they pour on the charm. Do you end up giving away money, gifts, sex, all of the above or something else? When someone is playing you, they want something. If you want some advice on how to not be manipulated, here is a rule of thumb: *do not loan* anything *to* anyone *you are dating!!* Now these people can be very crafty when they are trying to benefit from you. You are going to hear about how they are out of work, sick, have sick family members, have a broken-down car, just got out of a bad relationship, weren't loved by their parents, or recently had to bury their beloved dog… you name it! A manipulator is not above digging into the dirtiest cesspool of lies in order to get what they want from you.

When your boo or wannabe boo is telling you about all of these terrible events they are experiencing, give them your compassion. Give them your prayers and verbal support.

I'm Knot Ready

Some folks won't come out and ask you for your help. They will set you up with the sad story and expect you to offer the solution. Don't do it! Let them know, "I am so sorry to hear that. I will be praying that things get better for you." When that suggestive commentary doesn't work though, some will outright ask you for what they want. Most times it's money or something with a monetary value. Again, this is a no, no and a red flag! Let them know you are not able to give them whatever it is they are asking for. If they come back stating they know you have this or that, again, *red flag*! Tell them you are not comfortable giving or loaning them anything, it has nothing to do with what you have. Now the conversation with a true user will go in one of two directions at this point. Either they will really pour on the details of the sad story, trying to make you feel guilty about not helping, or they will retaliate with anger, blaming you for their situation not getting better. Their situation is not your problem and you are not responsible for saving them. When and if money or other valuables come into play, it should be after you've been in an established relationship together for a good amount of time (well over a year) and it should be a very rare if not isolated occurrence if it happens.

I know for some of you this is difficult because you are constantly getting walked over. I want you to know you need to learn how to stand up for yourself and introduce one very important word into your vocabulary. "no." It's that simple. You need to learn how to use your "no." It will save you so much trouble and if you get it right, the users will fall back on their own. You see, in some kind of way these people can smell an opportunity. And while I discussed money, it may very well *not* be money that they are after. They might be after an easy lay from someone who is vulnerable and needs someone to care about them. The people they are looking for will not put up much of a fight and will give up sex as quickly as they tell a person

I'm Knot Ready

their name. Sex is everything to some people, and the more of it they can get, the better they feel about themselves. Honey, you cannot get married to the person who is using you for money, sex or anything else. I say this because this person *will* marry you. This person *will* marry you and continue to use you for a roof over their heads and all the benefits that come with being with you. It's called self-preservation, my dear. While, for me and you, marriage may be a sacred, honorable gift to be cherished, there are millions of people in the world who couldn't care less, and I mean just that. They don't have the same mentality about marriage. These are not the people you want to convince that you would make a great spouse. (You shouldn't be looking to convince anyone of this, actually. The *one* should want you because of you. But the user is not looking for a spouse.) This is not the person you want to argue and fight with about making things official because of the ten kids and ten years you two have been together. Honey, marriage is not a priority for this person. This person could not be more wrong for you and what your heart needs in terms of a true companion and a lifelong mate. Can you say, "unhappily married"?

During this time in your relationship you will see this person that may one day become your spouse for who he is. You will see the good, bad, ugly, boring, fun, endearing and irritating. Getting married will not change you or your partner overnight. You will have the same height, weight, personality and behaviors you had the day before you exchanged vows. Your partner's morals and values are likely to remain the same for the rest of their lives. Over time, living together day after day will allow different behaviors to surface between you two as you are learning to live with one another. You will realize which one of you is the neat freak. You will realize who is the disciplinarian with the children. You will learn who takes longer to get ready, who gets hangry quicker and so on. This time you are spending with each other before you get married is contributing to your foundation. It is what you should be careful and precise at building in order to withstand all that is to come until the day you die. The foundation you create with this person is of the utmost importance because there is no way to foresee what challenges lie ahead. You will need to find safety and trust in the person you chose as your spouse. You will need them to be someone who can make decisions on your behalf when you are unavailable or unable to decide for yourself. You will need someone who's integrity and moral compass will keep you afloat. This is where you also learn things about yourself as it pertains to being in a meaningful relationship. When your heart is being cared for and you feel safe, how do you function? How do you behave and what compromises do you make? Have you had the conversation with yourself that reassures you it is ok to let your guard down with this person? Do you remind yourself to choose your battles when you are about to go ballistic about the dirty dishes or the overflowing trash? When you can see positive changes within yourself that you want to make, this person just might be good for you. And you know what? You just might be ready to be married.

Patience My Friend… Patience

Galatians Chapter 5

22 But the fruit of the Spirit is love, joy, peace, forbearance, kindness, goodness, faithfulness, **23** gentleness and self-control. Against such things there is no law. (NIV)

2 Corinthians Chapter 6

14 Do not be yoked together with unbelievers. For what do righteousness and wickedness have in common? Or what fellowship can light have with darkness? **15** What harmony is there between Christ and Belial? Or what does a believer have in common with an unbeliever? (NIV)

Chapter Five Reflection

1. How I felt before reading this chapter:

   _____
   _____
   _____

2. My feelings after having read this chapter:

   _____
   _____
   _____

3. I have to admit I can work on:

   _____
   _____
   _____

4. Things that have been going well because of my patience:

   _____
   _____
   _____

Chapter 6

Friends & Family

Let's switch gears a little. While you are getting your mind together thinking about how to be a good spouse, I want you to think about certain outside factors that have been harmful to your past relationships. Whether you'd like to admit it or not, family and friends play a role in many a couple's demise. I will start by saying this: friends and family are incredibly important. We all want our significant other to get along with the most important people in our lives. We want our family and friends to not only get along with our partner but also to approve of them. We want to hear the words, "Well done! What a keeper!"

Most times we do receive the approval we desire at the beginning of the relationship, when everyone still has their "new car" smell. It's after things aren't so new anymore that the problems begin. When we get comfortable in our relationships and start to deal with the real-life issues that come along, we naturally look to our family and friends for support. I think we can all say we have been "guilty" of this at some point in time within our relationships, some more than others. The issue, however, is when family and friends know too much of your business. When you are constantly running to certain people for their input and it affects how you show up in your relationship, that's a problem. "Well, Tina said this and Chris said that." If you are someone who feels like you need an outside opinion on the matters of your relationship on a regular basis, I'd like to encourage you to think about a few things.

First, consider the person you're confiding in. Are they successful in their own relationships? Have they shown the capacity to truly share mature, unbiased advice when you need it? Are they able to receive the information you share and keep it to themselves no matter what, or are they going to tell someone else with the disclaimer, "Don't tell anyone, I'm not supposed to say anything?" I think if you start here, you may realize when certain people have been privy to too much of your relationship business in the past. I think it is natural to want to share what's going well and what's going poorly, but you have to take into account that everyone is not capable of handling your news the way you need. If your go-to friend, Tina can't wait to get off the phone with you to tell someone else what is happening in your life, you need to make the decision now that Tina can no longer be your go-to.

Another thing to consider is while you are venting and explaining how your boo disappointed you and angered you by doing this and that, your confidante is more than likely judging him or her. Don't blame them—they can't help it! It shouldn't be a surprise that your loved ones have a problem hearing about someone mistreating or upsetting you. Think about it like this: when you have been on the

Mama Jr.

receiving end of a friend's love woes, didn't you feel less than favorably toward the person they described? The person who disrespected your friend, who cheated on them, who was ungrateful of them, who used or manipulated them… Uh huh! now it's coming back to you. We all want a non-judgmental listening ear, but we don't always know how to lend one. This is why it is important to decipher who gets to know your business…and guess what? There may be *no one*. Yep, there may not be anyone in your life who you share your relationship concerns with.

In a perfect world, I would suggest you speak with your partner about the issues you have with them. However, I am realistic in understanding if it were that simple, there would be no issues. If you don't have a true confidante, try confiding in yourself. Write things down in a journal or write a letter to the friend that you are trying to resist calling, and when you've had a chance to calm down, reread what you've written and see if anything comes up that will help you see the situation from a different point of view. You can also pretend the letter you've written is from a friend asking *you* for advice and think about how you would advise them.

If you don't feel as if you can be your own confidante, another option is to write anonymously to an advice column (i.e. my YouTube Channel). You can even do a Google search for your question and see what random opinions surface! There is information on Google for just about everything these days.

Another suggestion is to consider sharing your situation with a counselor or therapist. They will have an unbiased opinion, though some of you only want to be told what you want to hear. If this is the case (and while I don't recommend it) go ahead and tell your busy-body friend just to have your needs met for the moment. She'll tell you that you're right, he's a jerk and you deserve better. You'll feel empowered and right, but know that some of everybody is

Mama Jr.

going to know your troubles very soon, *and* you may not have actually received the best advice. Oh, and don't forget how you just betrayed your partner's trust by throwing him under the bus with your one-sided rant to your friend! So, you decide: confide in that friend, or try something more responsible this time around. You know what you've done in the past and it wasn't cool then and it will not be cool for your next relationship. You need to begin to learn how to do things differently if you want different results.

Some of us simply need to learn to keep our mouths shut and keep folks out of our personal affairs. We are so used to sharing every single thought with someone via phone, text or social media and we don't realize when it comes to our relationships, we have to do things entirely different in order to demonstrate honor and loyalty.

I know my suggestions may seem extreme when all you want to do is blow off a little steam, but it is important for your marriage that you learn to be a thoughtful partner.

I'm Knot Ready

Being thoughtful when you're angry allows you to make sure things aren't uncomfortable at the next family gathering. Having some self control now is more important than telling anyone who would listen how you couldn't get any help with the housework.

Think about it this way: is whatever this person has done a deal-breaker? I ask because *that* is when you may truly need a serious confidante to help you think clearly about your next decision. If the offense is (or could be) serious in nature and you do choose to share it with someone close to you, swear them to secrecy. Make sure you remind them of how very serious this situation is and if it ever comes back to you, you'll know they shared it and you will also never confide in them again. I say this because there will absolutely be times when you truly just want to get another person's take on a situation. I still caution you to be careful when deciding to share though, because you may end up working things out with your partner while your confidante

Mama Jr.

is stuck in the " I know what you did" mode as it pertains to your partner. You will move on and forgive your partner, but your friend won't be able to get past what they know. This is when you notice how that confidante starts giving your partner the side-eye and pursed lips whenever they come around. This is when the negative mumbling comments come into play. "Dirty sum ma ma mother." This is when they start reminding you of how you should be careful because of that one time. This isn't new news. I'm sure you've either been on the receiving or giving end of these examples. I am here to remind you that when you were, it was no fun for anyone, and you ended up being caught in the middle because you *had* to tell someone about how angry you were.

I remember when I separated from my ex-husband. I didn't tell my family about the things that I was going through that led to my separation. I didn't tell them until I had actually separated and was sure that he and I were not getting back together. My family was shocked because they had no idea things were bad with us, and they especially didn't realize it was bad enough for us to be divorcing. When I finally told them, I was strong enough to stand by the decision I had made. I didn't share my issues because the people in my family (including myself) always have an opinion, especially when there's drama involved. I didn't want other people's opinions telling me what I needed to do. I didn't want to explain the details and I didn't want anyone bashing him. Even now, there are still many details I have not shared with them, because my relationship was not their business. I had to decide what was going to be best for me without opinions that might sway me to do something that was best for my family and not for me. This was a difficult decision on my part because many days I hurt alone. I wanted badly to tell someone what I was going through, but I was confused, hurt and embarrassed, so I

Mama Jr.

thought it was best to keep it to myself. My confidante was God.

I'm not telling you to do what I did when bad times show up in your relationship. I am, however, telling you not to be self-centered and narrow minded, because this is a new ballgame, my dear. You are learning to be someone's spouse. There is honor and respect in this position. You need to keep your friends and family in a separate place that does not bleed over into your marriage.

Now, just like you don't throw mud on your spouse for everything they do that irritates you, you don't need to tell every good thing that happens in your relationship either. Here's the part when you think, *Say what?* Yep, I know how it sounds and I am not telling you to keep your relationship a secret. I am not telling you *not* to brag on how awesome your mate is from time to time, but you also need to be careful about how you do it and to who you brag to, for two reasons. ***Jealousy*** and ***Envy***. Familiar with these two, are ya? Uh huh, me too.

Look, I have not sugar-coated anything for you so far and I am not about to start now. The truth of the matter is, everyone is not happy for you and some want what you have... badly! Now pump your brakes! I never said this is how *everyone* is, but you would be surprised and even hurt to learn of those in your circle who have these feelings towards you. If you tell every amazing thing your partner does, some will get tired of hearing it. "She thinks Jimmy's crap doesn't stink!", "I'm tired of hearing about Jimmy." "Jimmy this, Jimmy that!" or, "Jimmy has it going on, I may have to see what he's about for myself."

Now, I will take this moment to thank my Father God in heaven that I have never had to deal with that last example. (at least not that I know of), but I have heard of people "hating" on someone because they were tired of hearing about someone's accomplishments and good attributes. If you need to boast about Jimmy, tell Jimmy how awesome he is or thank God for sending you a person who does the things that Jimmy does! I don't post a picture of every bouquet of flowers that my boyfriend gets me or every gift he buys, and I don't boast about every thoughtful thing that he says and does. I am very happy with the way he treats me, but this is *our* relationship. We are not celebrities on a reality show. I want to enjoy our relationship without an audience.

While I want you— no, I *need* you to find a respectful balance as to how to include your family and friends within your relationship, I also want you to know when all gloves are off and to seek their solace. When you are in a relationship with someone who is not good for you, you will find your family and friends offering their input before you even ask for it. This may have nothing to do with what you have said to them, but rather be due to something they saw or heard. Like I said before, no one you love wants to see you be mistreated. If no one knows you are in an unhappy or abusive relationship, someone needs to know. They need to know because if anything happens to you or your children, someone needs to be able to tell the police that you and your partner had issues and tell them that they need to question your partner.

Most times, people in bad relationships are the ones who guard their relationships with their lives. They don't want anyone to know they are dealing with a bad partner because people will tell them to leave and, for one reason or several, this person does not want to leave the relationship or they do not feel like they safely *can* leave. If you are dealing with a person who is disrespectful or abusive in any way, you need some help. I say "you need help" instead of advising you to leave the relationship because these two things are not deal-breakers for everyone.

Let me be clear. If your partner is abusive and/or disrespectful when you're dating them, do *not* marry this person. Marriage is not going to fix them. The way a person treats you before you say, " I do" is going to be the way they treat you afterward. You have come too far to allow yourself to be stuck with someone that doesn't appreciate all you have to offer. If for whatever reason, you don't know how to get out of the situation or don't want to get out of the situation, call the domestic abuse hotline at 1-800-799-SAFE (7233) or go online to www.thehotline.org. This is a twenty-four-hour service and there are trained staff available to talk to you about whatever you're experiencing. If you don't like the information the staff gives you, you can hang up or log off. *It's anonymous and it's free.*

You already know you want better, and I want you to figure out how to make those first steps. If you are in a relationship that is toxic or unhealthy and you do not know how to leave and things are not getting better, please reach out to the domestic abuse hotline.

I'm Knot Ready

Please remember this: friends and family mean well but they do not always give us the best wisdom or advice. You know if you've allowed a loved one to become too involved in your past relationships or not. If so, this is something you need to admit now, and you need to decide that it will not happen going forward in order to have a healthy marriage. Making this declaration does not mean you won't need someone to talk to when issues arise within your marriage. You will, however, have to decide how to get the support you need and remain true to your commitment to your spouse at the same time. This is why I said earlier your foundation is important in how you deal with one another. If, while in your dating stage, you ran and told others all of your partner's business, you will not stop just because you're married. You have to set the tone of how your relationship will work and how you will or will not allow others to be involved. Sure, some will try to get information from you about what's going on with you two, but you have to let them know it is not something you are not comfortable sharing. You have to let them know your marital issues are not up for discussion and you have to stand by your word. It may not be initially received well by those who are used to gossiping with you, but eventually they will realize you mean what you say. It may even rub off on them and they will start to make some changes with how they operate within their relationships!

When you get married, most times the vows include some variation of "forsaking all others as long as you both shall live." Decide what that means to you and how you will demonstrate this in your marriage. I don't know about you but I have never had to take an oath on forsaking others for my siblings, friends, aunts, uncles or cousins! I know putting your spouse before family may feel uncomfortable if you are used to operating a certain way, but that's what this book has been about: challenging the way you have been doing things and realizing there may be a more effective way to make things happen.

Chapter Six Reflection

1. How my family and friends have been involved in my previous/current relationship:

   _____
   _____
   _____

2. I can admit these things need to improve:

   _____
   _____
   _____

3. What I learned from reading this chapter:

   _____
   _____
   _____

4. I know family and friends will not be an issue in my marriage because:

   _____
   _____
   _____

Friends & Family

Mark Chapter 10

7 For this reason a man will leave his father and mother and be united to his wife **8** and the two will become one flesh. So they are no longer two, but one flesh. **9** Therefore, what God has joined together, let no one separate. (NIV)

Chapter 7

Are You Marriage Material?

What is "marriage material"? Think about what that means to you. Does it mean someone who is ready to cook and clean or fix things around the house and take out the trash? Does it mean someone who is ready to commit to one person forever and will proudly tell others the same? Maybe. It may mean all of these things or none of them. I think it means whatever you want it to mean.

As I mentioned before, no matter what type of person you are and whatever you bring to the table, someone is looking for just that. My definition of someone who is marriage material may never look like your definition, and vice versa. The only thing that matters is if the person who wants to marry you feels like you are right for them. I will, however, say in my opinion, all marriages should have some of the same ingredients, just like if you were baking a cake. No matter what type of cake you make (unless you are adhering to dietary restrictions), it will have eggs, flour, sugar and milk. After that, all sorts of things can be added to make a variety of wonderful treats. Marriage is the same way. I feel that all marriages need to have certain ingredients before adding other things. I believe those basic ingredients for marriage include love, loyalty, respect, and communication.

Now, just like some people will argue that you can make a cake without sugar, some will argue that my four ingredients aren't needed within a marriage. And maybe they're not for you, but I am no more interested in a sugar-free cake than I am interested in a disrespectful marriage! I am well aware there is no template for a happy marriage. Every marriage is going to be different because the people are different. As human beings however, we all have some of the same basic needs and this is why I listed those four necessary attributes above. I believe if you want to be marriage material, you should at least come to the relationship with those four things, and you should make it your business that your partner also comes to the relationship with the same. While you are dating, those attributes should be demonstrated and strengthened as you invest more time into one another. So many people are disrespectful, disloyal and unloving within their relationships and wonder why they are not married to their partner yet! I don't understand why folks are in a relationship with these types of people to begin with, but that's another story.

When you say you want to get married, you should understand that the person who accepts your hand in marriage is looking for you to be loyal, loving and respectful whether they have actually said these things to you or not. Communication is probably the most important thing of all, but we know many relationships suffer because of miscommunication.

Think about your interaction with your previous or current partner. Think about how you speak to them. Do you put them down, curse at them and constantly belittle them? Are you dishonest or disloyal? If you do treat your partner this way, or have treated previous partners this way in the past, you have to ask yourself why this person (or anyone) would want to marry you. Do you speak to strangers better than you speak to your partner? Are you more patient with others than you are with him? Do you say the first gut-wrenching, hurtful thing that comes to mind because you're upset? What is it about you that should make this person feel like their heart is safe with you?

Yes, your partner should feel and know they are safe with you! Do you remember how I Corinthians 13:4-7 explained love?

> **4** Love is patient, love is kind. It does not envy, it does not boast, it is not proud. **5** It does not dishonor others, it is not self-seeking, it is not easily

angered, it keeps no record of wrongs. **6** Love does not delight in evil but rejoices with the truth. **7** It always protects, always trusts, always hopes, always perseveres. (NIV)

If you have (or are currently) handling your significant other in a manner less than what is described above, my dear, please stop calling it love! You can be honest and loving and gentle and patient and grow with your significant other without tearing them down. People like to blame their mistreatment of others on "tough love", but guess what? Tough love is still *love*! You don't have to be a jerk to let a person know you disagree with them or are bothered by something they have said or done. You don't have to emasculate or dishonor your man in order to put your foot down about a topic. You don't get to redefine love because you haven't figured out how to execute it as it was intended.

Now, if you have gone into defensive mode thinking about all you have bought this person over the years or the roof you put over their head, *stop it!* Not everyone can be bought. Your partner may allow you to take care of their material needs, but they still desire someone to take care of their heart, and until you learn to do this they are not going to be running to put a ring on your finger. Being weak and being submissive are two entirely different things! You can be a strong and submissive woman.

I want you to understand the way you interact with your partner is so very important. Be careful with their heart because the way you handle it demonstrates how you will treat it when you take their hand in marriage. Be careful with the words you use and how you deliver them. This is your chance to practice being their spouse. You should treat them better than anyone else in this world. There should be no one alive that gets to disrespect your spouse, including you! If you feel like, "I'm not going to coddle and sugar coat anything. I should be able to be myself." Okay, but how's that working out for you? Let me also ask you this. When you think about the marriage you'd like to be in, do you think about shouting, cursing, arguing, crying, and sadness? I honestly hope you said, "no". If not, what do you think will be the result of handling your spouse with anger, disrespect, dishonor and disloyalty? You cannot give your spouse whatever pitiful, emotional, angry version of yourself you decide will show up on any given day and expect them to be happy with it. I don't expect you to be a phony with an apron on and a smile, but the way you show up in your relationship absolutely matters. I do expect you to communicate like an adult with the person you want to spend the rest of your life with. I expect you to say, "The way you flirted with the waitress during dinner made me uncomfortable. It was disrespectful and I would appreciate it if it never happens again." We all know that type of conversation could get much more colorful with a few curse words and some interesting threats depending on the person speaking, but that is just not the way to handle things. When your normal interaction is like this, it can be toxic and being in a toxic relationship should never be an option.

If you have issues to address within yourself, address them. At least be working at bettering yourself! People want peace when they come home. I know I do! People want to feel safe and secure. Where does peace and security come from with a partner who is always combative? Why should a person have to walk on eggshells in their own home because they don't know how you're going to blow up at them today? Be mindful of how you are in relationships now and ask yourself, "Am I marriage material?" If you want to be married, now is the time to get yourself under control and start acting like it.

I wanted to address this because I shudder when I hear the way some couples speak to one another. They say the most

Mama Jr.

hurtful things in the heat of the moment because they want to be right or win their arguments. I understand that people will argue. I understand people are going to get angry. I understand how passions run high about certain topics, but there is never a time when you get to disrespect and berate your partner. If both of you hold these rules as a standard, you are at least protecting the other's heart when you tell them hard truths, like they are spending too much money or you need more support about your career goals.

I want to reiterate this is not a game. This "marriage thing" you said you want is hard work, and hopefully, after reading this book, you can understand there is work to be done even if you haven't met your boo-to-be. Marriage is not for the weak, and *yes!* Only the strong survive.

The Bible tells us when a man and a woman get married, "the two become one." If you disrespect your partner, you are disrespecting yourself. If you take the time to get to know your partner, you will learn how they handle stress, anger, frustration, disappointment and rejection. You should communicate to them what your triggers are, your partner should communicate theirs, and both of you should respect those triggers and make a personal oath to yourselves to never activate those triggers. After your disagreements are over, you still want them to be your partner.

I know this type of self reflection is never easy because you have to admit when there are some changes that need to be made. We all want to believe we are the best thing ever, but the truth is we are all a work in progress. I haven't been in an argument with a partner in a very long time, but I can recall being that loud, disrespectful, neck-rolling beast when I became upset. I felt terrible about some of the things I said afterwards, but at the time, I needed to be right. I had to learn that disagreements are not about being right. Disagreements are going to happen with people in general, so they are bound to happen when you live with someone every single day. My marriage should've been about God. Instead, I made those disagreements about me. I was in no way, shape or form trying to honor God with the things I said.

I now know it is so very crucial to choose a partner I can be vulnerable with instead of trying to be right. I know the way I treat my husband should be a reflection of the way the Lord wants me to treat him. If I have been trusted to be a man's wife, then the Lord is counting on me to treat him a certain way. My husband is God's child and I know God doesn't want me to mistreat his child. I'm not trying to deal with the consequences of that! I should conduct myself with the utmost respect in or outside of my husband's presence. When I am a wife, I will choose to conduct myself with integrity and respect my husband, because that is what God expects of me. My husband will benefit from those personal choices I have made to be a virtuous wife, and I will be blessed to have chosen the hand of an upstanding man who will make his own God-honoring choices.

Are You Marriage Material?

Ephesians Chapter 5

25 Husbands, love your wives, just as Christ loved the church and gave himself up for her **26** to make her holy, cleansing her by the washing with water through the word, **27** and to present her to himself as a radiant church, without stain or wrinkle or any other blemish, but holy and blameless. **28** In this same way, husbands ought to love their wives as their own bodies. He who loves his wife loves himself. **29** After all, no one ever hated their own body, but they feed and care for their body, just as Christ does the church— **30** for we are members of his body. (NIV)

I Corinthians Chapter 13

4 Love is patient, love is kind. It does not envy, it does not boast, it is not proud. **5** It does not dishonor others, it is not self-seeking, it is not easily angered, it keeps no record of wrongs. **6** Love does not delight in evil but rejoices with the truth. **7** It always protects, always trusts, always hopes, always perseveres.

I Corinthians Chapter 16

14 Do everything in love. (NIV)

Chapter Seven Reflection

1. I know I am marriage material because:

   _____
   _____
   _____

2. After reading this chapter, I realize:

   _____
   _____
   _____

3. I have to admit I can work on:

   _____
   _____
   _____

4. As it pertains to my current/future relationship, I am proud to say:

   _____
   _____
   _____

Conclusion

Marriage is special for so many reasons. I don't know about you, but as a woman, it puts me on top of the world to know my man wants to marry me. It means he is choosing me. It means I am the one person in his life he actually wants to have by his side forever. What an honor! A person can't choose their parents, siblings or other relatives. Sure, they choose their friends, but there is no ceremony to commemorate the occasion. For my man to have spent a certain amount of time with me and come to the conclusion he wants more of the same forever is just so humbling. Accepting me for who I am, where I come from, and what I represent is the most flattering gesture of them all.

Maybe this is why it is also the most challenging relationship one can have. Because it *is* a choice. You know

Mama Jr.

your brother is always going to be your brother, so you don't worry about it when you don't see eye to eye. But your spouse... you *do* get to choose your spouse, which means there is so much more at stake. You choose to build a family with this person. You choose to share your experiences, your emotions, your fears and insecurities. You choose to love and laugh with this person throughout all of life's surprises.

I believe that marriage is the ultimate choice in life. This is why I wanted to pull you to the side and ask you to take it more seriously, because while this is what marriage means to me, it may not mean any of those things to the person who ends up asking me to marry him. He may have his own wonderful reasons for asking me to be his wife, but they may not look anything like mine. While that may be all well and good, I at least want to make sure we are on the same page as far as what marriage means to the other person. I want to make sure my husband knows how important this covenant is to me and I want to make sure he isn't just trying to lock in a permanent place to stay!

This is why we have to change how we operate within our relationships. People in relationships often have a different understanding of where they stand with one another, which allows years of miscommunication and frustration as each wonders why the other person hasn't met their needs. What they don't realize is they have *never* been on the same page! People don't have the hard conversations that they should be having in the beginning of their relationships because they are too busy "liking" one another. By the time that wears off, years have gone by and resentment has built up because the relationship has not grown in the way either person has expected.

I wanted to ask you to not be fooled with the movies and social media examples of marriage, because there's so much more to it than that. Marriage is a gamble. You have no idea if the other person is going to live up to your expectations, but you choose to roll the dice on them anyway.

I want you to continue to want marriage. I want you to continue to hold on to the idea that you would be great at it. I also want you to be aware of the absolutely bumpy ride it is, and I want you to do all you can to prepare to stay on it until the wheels fall off. I don't want you to go into it thinking there's an escape hatch when things get too uncomfortable.

Please take some time to get to know yourself. Do what you can to address and heal your past hurts no matter where they came from. Also, please take some time to get to know the person you believe may be the one for you. Once you get married, you deserve to have it last forever. Please trust God and ask him to guide you as you are beginning a journey whose outcome only He knows.

I pray you have been empowered, motivated and inspired by this book. I pray you are able to receive the words in this book as I intended them: with love. I appreciate you for allowing me to be myself and have fun with this project. Thank you so much for your support.

Mama Jr.

www.ingramcontent.com/pod-product-compliance
Lightning Source LLC
Chambersburg PA
CBHW020908080526
44589CB00011B/498